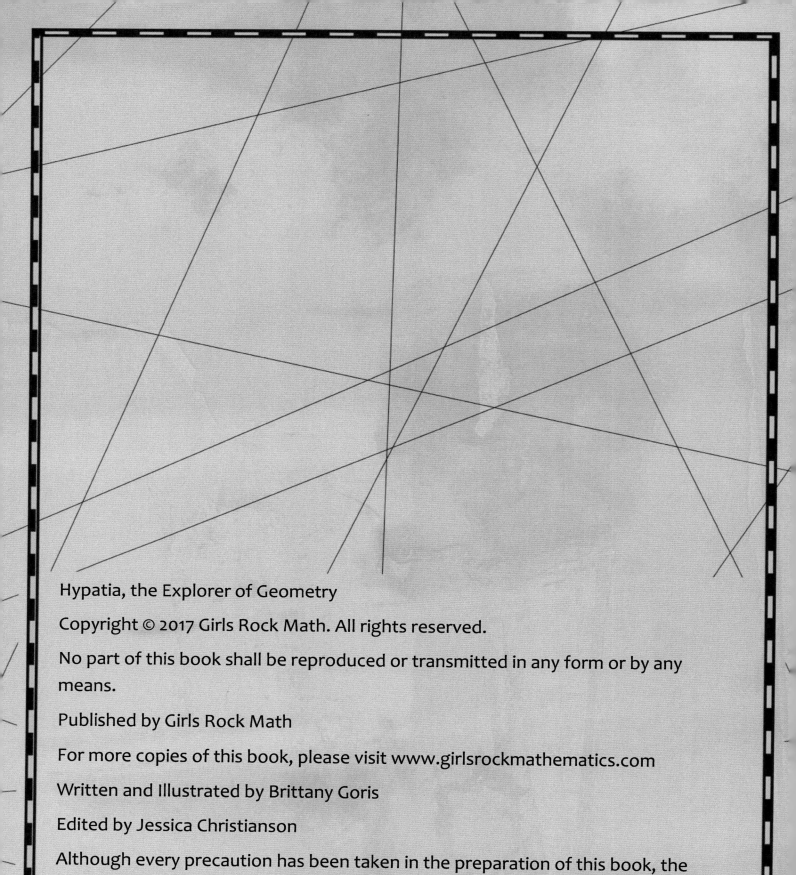

Hypatia, the Explorer of Geometry

Copyright © 2017 Girls Rock Math. All rights reserved.

No part of this book shall be reproduced or transmitted in any form or by any means.

Published by Girls Rock Math

For more copies of this book, please visit www.girlsrockmathematics.com

Written and Illustrated by Brittany Goris

Edited by Jessica Christianson

Although every precaution has been taken in the preparation of this book, the publisher and author assume no responsibility for errors or omissions. Neither is any liability assumed for damages resulting from the use of information contained herein.

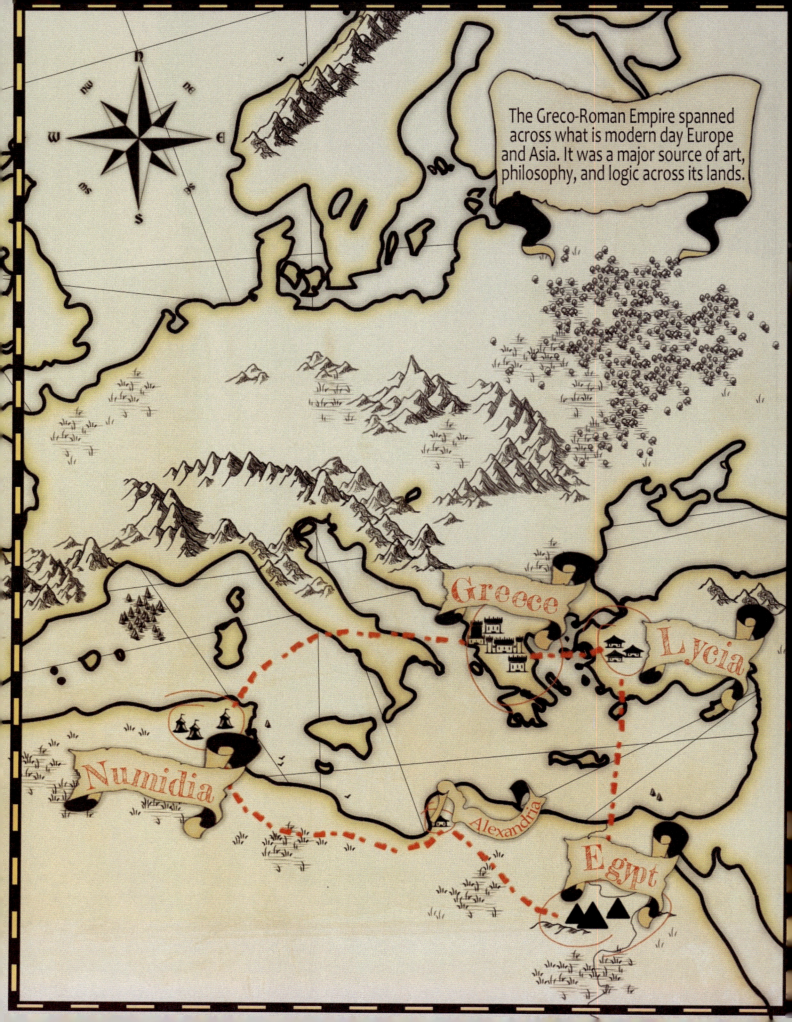

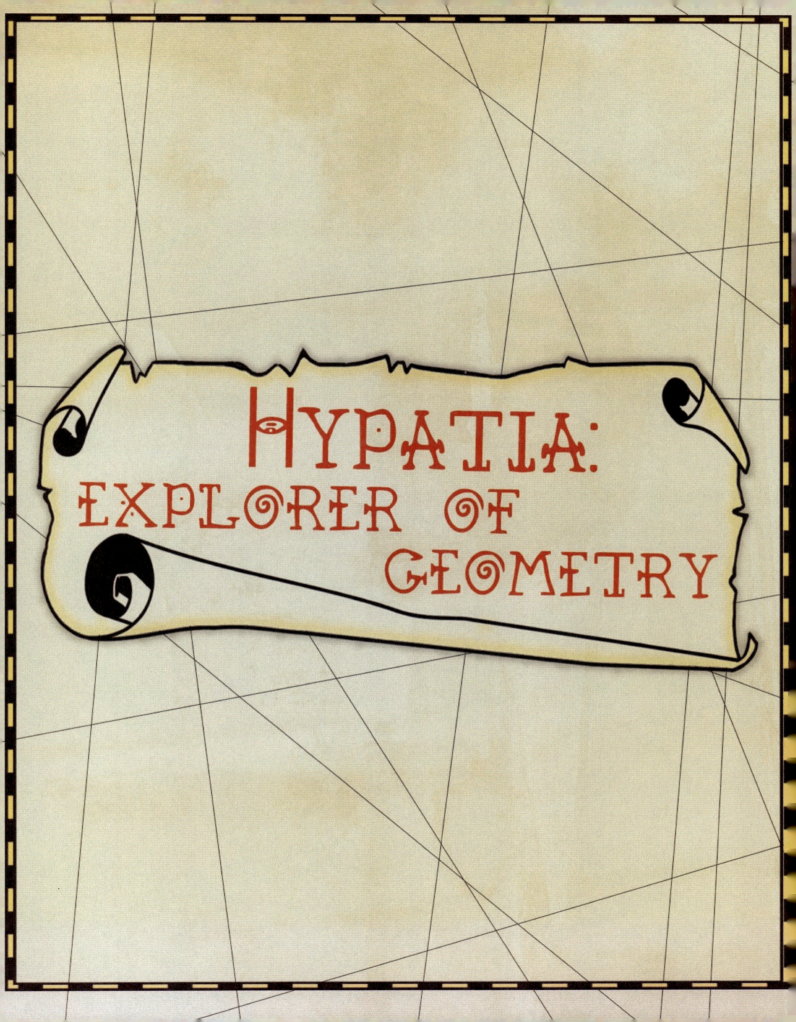

The constellation Orion shines brightly in the starry skies over Egypt. The three stars of Orion's belt each shine upon the three points of the largest pyramids in all of Egypt. It was under these bright stars that a little girl named Hypatia was born over a thousand years ago.

Hypatia lived in an important city called Alexandria. Back then Alexandria was ruled by the Greeks and Romans. The cultures of the ancient worlds intertwined and all of the great thinkers and scholars would gather there at the Library of Alexandria. It was a special place that held all of the world's knowledge at the time. Hypatia's father, Theon, was the head librarian. He was the keeper of the world's knowledge.

As a very young girl, Hypatia was bright and curious. She explored the halls of the great library, getting lost amid the fragile scrolls and the secret knowledge they held. Her vivid imagination took her on adventures without ever leaving the library. She would read about faraway places and wonder if she would ever see them in her lifetime. Her father saw how she gazed at the maps on the walls and the stars in the sky and knew he would never be able to keep her inside the walls of the great library. She was destined to be an adventurer.

Girls in ancient times didn't go to school. Luckily, the library was bigger and better than any school, so Theon began to teach her how to read and write. Hypatia's curiosity was nearly impossible to satisfy. After she learned Greek and Latin, she learned to read hieroglyphs , which was what the Ancient Egyptians used to write. She loved to study their mythology and learn of their gods such as Anubis and Ra.

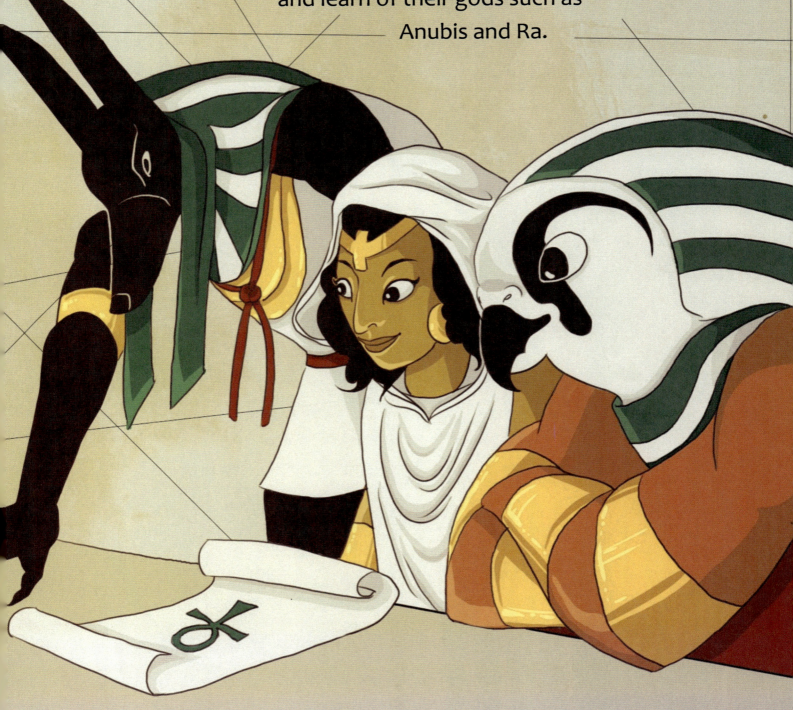

One day, Theon approached Hypatia with good news. He was asked to travel down the Nile River to the City of Giza, home of the great pyramids. There, he was to meet with a scholar who had found some scrolls to donate to the library. Usually he did these travels alone, but looking at his curious daughter, he knew she was ready to join him.

The journey was long, but Hypatia was in awe as they traveled along the Nile. There she saw animals like crocodiles and cranes, and gazed nightly at the stars in the bright open sky. After many days, they finally arrived at the great pyramids.

When they arrived at Giza, Hypatia saw the great pyramids looming over the horizon. Never before had she seen anything with such an unusual shape. Walking around the perimeter, she discovered something fascinating. The pyramids were simple shapes with four sides, and yet they were more impressive than anything she'd ever seen before. She asked her father, how had people been able to build something so huge?

Hypatia decided she wanted to learn math. As they made their way back home to Alexandria, Theon taught Hypatia all he knew about numbers. By the time they returned, Hypatia couldn't get numbers out of her mind!

Soon, Theon was asked to go on another long journey, this time across the Mediterranean Sea. Hypatia begged to go with him. She told him that now that she knew about numbers, she could help the sailors guide them across the sea. Theon admired his daughter's enthusiasm and knew she would enjoy the adventure.

They boarded a ship and ventured to Lycia, which is in what is now called Turkey. There they saw giant tombs cut out of rock in the hillside and again she was captivated by their architecture. They were decorated with so many shapes that she couldn't imagine people had built them, and so she asked her father, how had people been able to build something so detailed?

Now she had so many more questions about math. She knew about numbers, so as they headed back to Alexandria, Theon taught Hypatia all about shapes, lines, and angles. He taught her geometry.

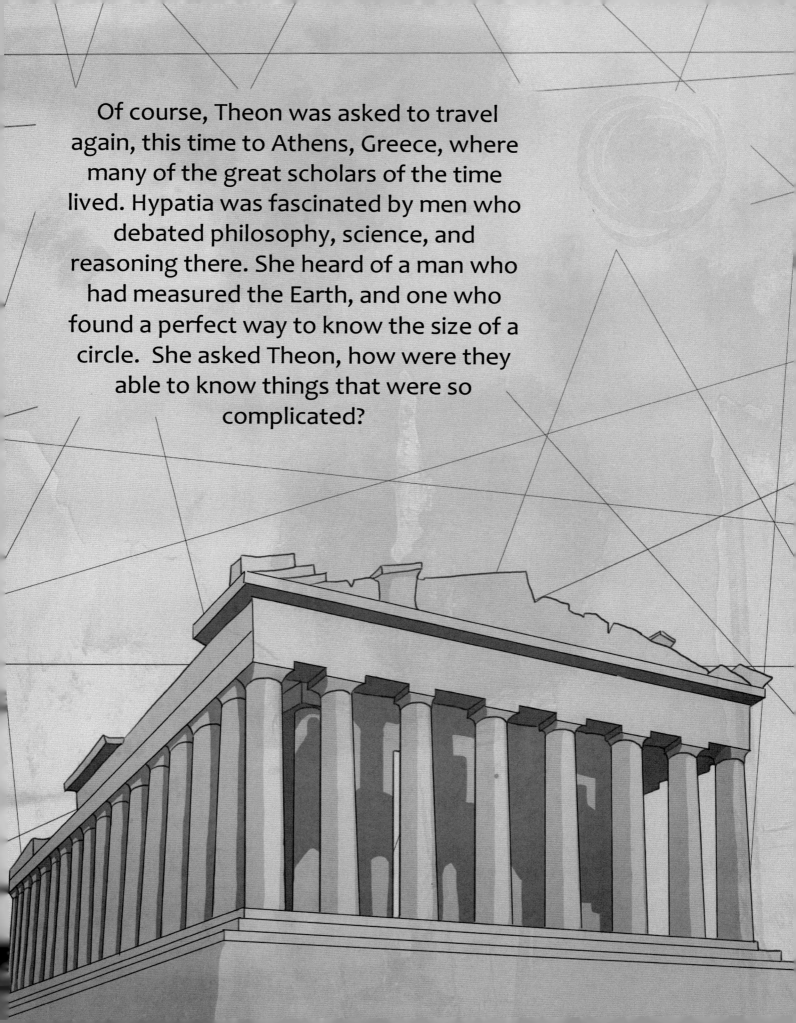

Of course, Theon was asked to travel again, this time to Athens, Greece, where many of the great scholars of the time lived. Hypatia was fascinated by men who debated philosophy, science, and reasoning there. She heard of a man who had measured the Earth, and one who found a perfect way to know the size of a circle. She asked Theon, how were they able to know things that were so complicated?

Theon told her the answer was math.

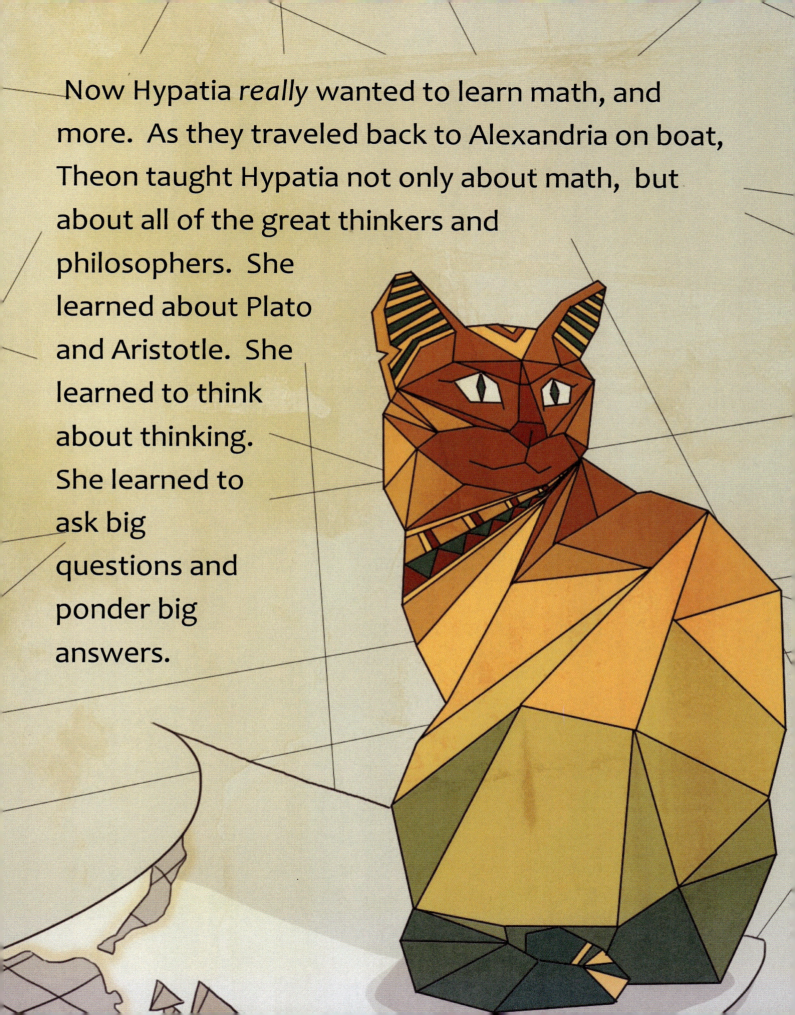

Now Hypatia *really* wanted to learn math, and more. As they traveled back to Alexandria on boat, Theon taught Hypatia not only about math, but about all of the great thinkers and philosophers. She learned about Plato and Aristotle. She learned to think about thinking. She learned to ask big questions and ponder big answers.

Theon was asked to travel to Numidia, in what is today Algeria. It was a place far different than any she'd been before. Their people were nomadic, meaning they didn't stay in one place, but rather moved their tribes around to follow the animals they ate. They were very skilled at riding horses, something Hypatia had never seen a woman do. For the first time she saw that not everyone had to live the same way. Her father asked her what she would like to spend her days doing.

As a scholar and professor, Theon encouraged Hypatia to study math, and also science, astronomy, and astrology. He taught her everything he knew, and then together they learned even more. Hypatia worked hard day and night to become not just a scholar like her father, but a mathematician like the Egyptians and Lycians, and a philosopher like the Greeks.

At the time just about all the mathematicians and learned people she met were men; few women even knew how to read or write! Hypatia felt lucky to have a father who believed she could do and be anything.

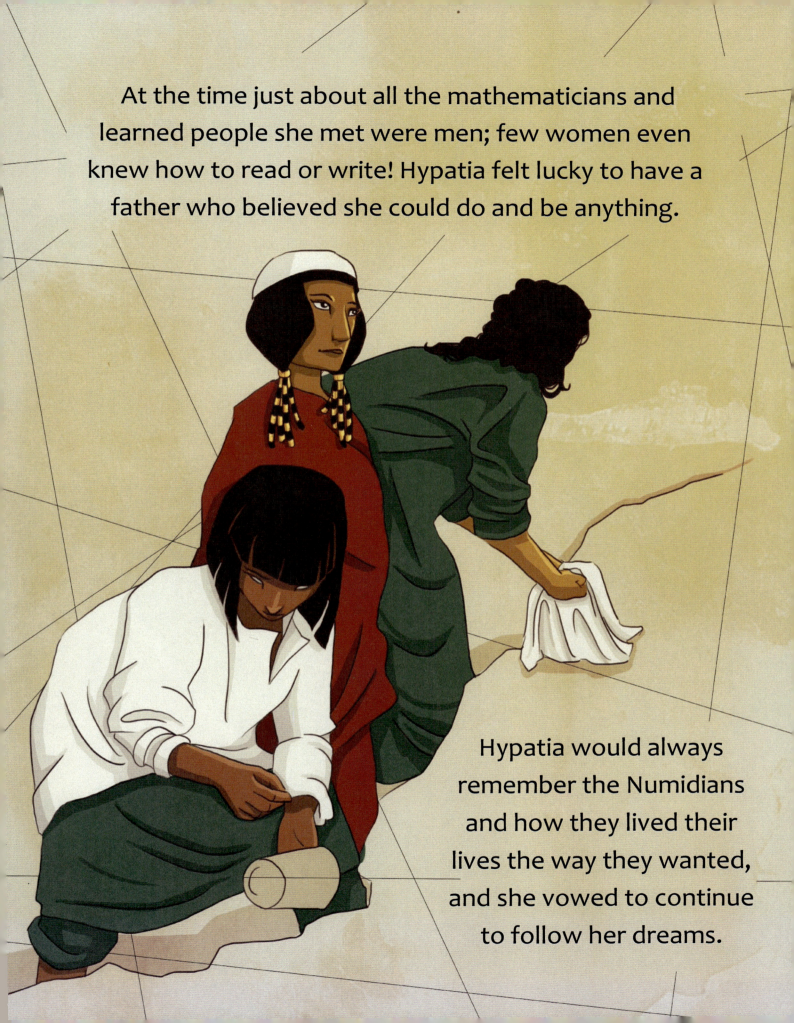

Hypatia would always remember the Numidians and how they lived their lives the way they wanted, and she vowed to continue to follow her dreams.

Hypatia began to explore what always fascinated her most, which was the math behind the shapes she saw around her. As an adult, she helped develop work on the Conics of Apollonius, which helped people understand parabolas, hyperbolas and ellipses (important mathematical shapes), which would change the way people understood math for centuries. She also became an inventor, and created something called an astrolabe which helped sailors use the stars to steer their ships in the right direction.

Hypatia also became a teacher, and had many students follow in her footsteps exploring the world of math and science. Her legacy as a wonderful teacher and thinker spread to many lands. When people had big questions about math, philosophy, or astronomy, they would travel nights and days to ask for help from the brilliant woman they called the Explorer of Geometry. She would often ponder these questions until a smile would come over her face, and in the words of her father she'd say, "The answer is math!"

TRY THIS: HEIROGLYPHIC ALPHABET

Learn how the Ancient Egyptians used Heiroglyphics, then decode the message on the next page!

STORY DISCUSSION:

1. How was Hypatia different from other girls growing up in ancient Alexandria?

2. For over a thousand years, people forgot about the story of Hypatia, even though she was the first female mathematician. Many male mathematicians were famous, had books written about them, and were taught about in school. Why do you think it took so long for people to start talking about her life story?

AFTERWORD:

What exactly is a mathematician anyway? At the most basic level, it's someone who does math. This means YOU are a mathematician! But a mathematician also spends a lot of her time learning about math, thinking about math, and using math to solve problems they see in the world around them. Hypatia was one of these early mathematicians.

People have been doing mathematics for almost as long as we can look back at human history. Archeologists have found bones used by early humans with notches in them used for counting.

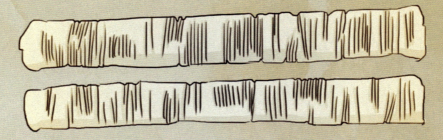

The Ishango bone, a tally stick from central Africa, dates from about 20,000 years ago

Egyptians had a method of doubling numbers that they used to solve multiplication problems and a method of dividing whole numbers to make simple fractions that seems much more complicated than how we use fractions today. But it worked for them! The ancient Egyptians used a base-10 number system, which you can see earlier in the story.

Hypatia lived in a time called the Greco-Roman period in Egypt, which lasted about 300 years. During this time, the Greeks and the Romans ruled Egypt. Famous stories like Antony and Cleopatra (the play by William Shakespeare) and stories of Alexander the Great come from this time. Both the Greeks and Romans had their own mathematics, inventions, and architecture and brought these ideas to the great city of Alexandria.

The Greeks are famous for coming up with some of the first ideas about geometry. Great thinkers like Pythagoras thought about angles, lines, and shapes. In geometry, one of the first lessons you'll learn is about the Pythagorean theorem, which helps us measure the sides of triangles. Interestingly, the Ancient Egyptians also knew about this, and used it to help them build their pyramids long before Pythagoras explained it!

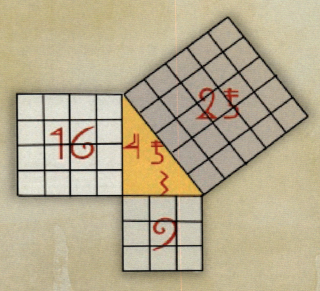

The Romans were most famous for Roman numerals, which we still use today. Clock faces often have Roman numerals. If you watch a movie all the way to the end credits, you'll see that films use Roman numerals to show the date the movie was made. One other place you see Roman numerals is sporting events, such as the Olympics or the Super Bowl. The Roman numeral system makes solving equations so complicated that most Romans did very little actual math. It would take a long time to solve even a pretty simple addition problem using Roman numerals!

Using Roman numerals, the sum 1,233 + 1,114 becomes:

   MCCXXIII + MCXIV
= MCXXIII + MCXIIII

```
      M    CC    XX    III
+     M    C     X     IIII
= MM  CCC  XXX   IIIIIII
```

Math has changed a lot since ancient times, but one thing is certain: all of the discoveries, changes, and learning around mathematics that have happened over the centuries have helped humans make amazing advances in science and engineering. Can you imagine a world without math?

BRITTANY GORIS

ABOUT THE AUTHOR

Hypatia: Explorer of Geometry was written and fully illustrated by Brittany Goris on behalf of Girls Rock Math. Girls Rock Math is an arts-based math camp that strives to provide thought-provoking, creative experiences in math, empowering girls to develop confidence in their skills and a life-long interest in mathematics.

Brittany is a writer, artist, and educator, who combines her passions in Girls Rock Math to help youth achieve their potential.

She loves finding creative ways like her stories and art to teach kids about mathematicians and role models in STEM fields.

In her free time she likes to rock climb, play board games, and cook vegetarian meals. *With support from Jessica Christianson*

Made in the USA
Middletown, DE
03 July 2021